To Ellie, Georgia and Van. Three little legends with VIP status.
—Mr Luke

To Wose, love you lots. Even when you win. Love Cwis.
—C.K.

Scholastic Australia
An imprint of Scholastic Australia Pty Limited
PO Box 579 Gosford NSW 2250
ABN 11 000 614 577
www.scholastic.com.au

Part of the Scholastic Group
Sydney • Auckland • New York • Toronto • London • Mexico City • New Delhi • Hong Kong • Buenos Aires • Puerto Rico

Published by Scholastic Australia in 2025.

A catalogue record for this book is available from the National Library of Australia

ISBN: 978-1-76164-271-5

Typeset in Bryant featuring Chaloops.

Printed in China by RR Donnelley.
Scholastic Australia's policy, in association with RR Donnelley, is to use papers that are renewable and made efficiently from wood from responsibly managed sources, so as to minimise its environmental footprint.

10 9 8 7 6 5 4 3 2 25 26 27 28 29 / 2

A Scholastic Australia Book

Mr Luke's Magic Library

Dinosaur Trail

Written by Mr Luke

Illustrated by Chris Kennett

The morning was buzzing, the mood was just right
for stories, adventures and books to delight.
The class lined up, excitement galore,
for today was **LIBRARY DAY**, their turn to explore!

Magic
Library

The shelves stood tall, with wonders untold,
and **MAGICAL STORIES,** both new ones and old.

'Mr Luke, we like this one!' they all had to agree.
A **DINOSAUR ADVENTURE**; what could it be?

They passed him the book with a giggle and grin,
hearts filled with wonder, adventures begin!
Would they trek through the trees or stomp through the clay?
The **MAGIC LIBRARY** could now take them away!

He opened the book and a rumble was heard,
the ground shook once, then twice, then a third!
With a flash of light, a **WHOOSH** and a **ROAR!**
They weren't in the library anymore!

They landed in a world so vast and wide
full of towering trees and mountains so high.
A prehistoric land, wild and free
with **DINOSAURS** as far as the eye could see!

As they roamed and explored, a voice rang out,
'Come quick! Look at this!' came Lauren's loud shout.
A **DINOSAUR EGG,** spotty and round.
Where was its home? Could it be found?

So they walked through the jungle, wild and wide,
and found a dino with a lumbering stride.
'Excuse me, sir, is this egg yours?'
TRICERATOPS frowned then after a pause . . .

'Too round! Too small! Ours aren't like that at all!
Try the trees, look up **HIGH**,
to the nests in the sky!'

The class climbed up, Mr Luke in the lead
to where the **BRACHIOSAURUS** liked to go feed.
'Excuse me, ma'am, is this egg for you?'
She took one look, then said what was true.

'Too light! Too bright! It doesn't seem right.
Go to the CLIFFS where the high-flyers nest,
where the wind is wild and where the egg might rest.'

The cliffs were steep and could not be scaled.
'We'll never reach that nest, I think we have failed.'
But then with a **SWOOSH!** And a flap and a glide,
some **PTERANODONS** swooped down and landed beside.

'We need to get up there; can you help us, please?
We've searched all around, through the jungle and trees.'
With a cheerful squawk and a dip of their heads,
they offered a **RIDE** to the clifftop beds.

The wind rushed past as
they reached the nest
where a **PTERANODON**
mum was having a rest.

'Excuse us, hello, we hope you don't mind.
Is this egg yours? It's been left behind.'

'Too smooth! Too spotted! Mine are striped, not dotted.
Try down on the **PLAINS,'** the mother explained.

Down on the plains, the ground gave a shake
and a giant **ROAR** made the class quake!
A **T-REX** appeared, teeth gleaming bright.
The class turned to run in a terrible fright!

In panic and fear, Mr Luke lost his grip.
The egg rolled from his hands with a wobble and flip.
The class froze in horror; not one made a sound.
The egg landed with a **CRACK!** Then rolled on the ground.

TAP TAP TAP came a sound from below.
The egg cracked some more,
something started to show.

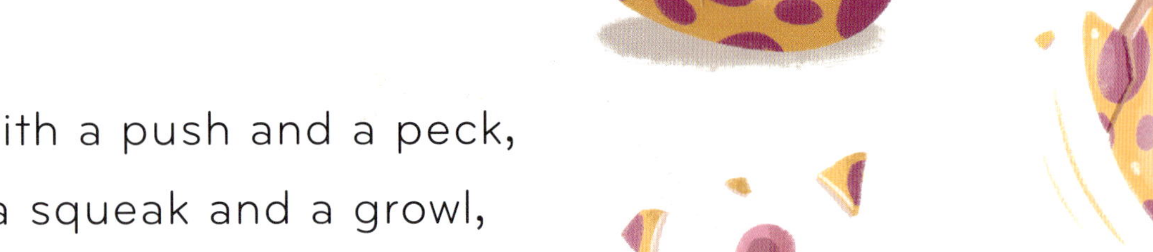

With a push and a peck,
a squeak and a growl,

a **BABY DINOSAUR**
made a wobbly howl.

The T-Rex looked as relieved as can be.
'My **LOST BABY** is back!' she roared with great glee.
The quest was complete, the mystery solved.
The class had helped; another story to be told!

Then the lunch bell rang, it was time to depart
and the book pulled them home with
a **MAGICAL SPARK!**
Back in the library, safe like before,
back to the school,
to the bookshelves once more.

'Where will we go next time? We all want to know!'
the class called out; they were ready to go.
Mr Luke laughed. 'We'll just wait and see!

The library is **MAGIC** and the books hold the key.'

With books, you can travel to places unknown.
Through JUNGLES, through TIME or to WORLDS of your own!